Donald Gaskins:

The Meanest Man in America

by Jack Rosewood

Historical Serial Killers and Murderers

True Crime by Evil Killers

Volume 7

Copyright © 2015 by Wiq Media

ALL RIGHTS RESERVED

No part of this book may be reproduced, stored in a retrieval system, or transmitted in any form or by any means, electronic, mechanical, photocopying, recording, scanning, or otherwise, without the prior written permission of the publisher.

ISBN-13: 978-1517756024

Introduction

Psychiatrists, psychologists, and social scientists have all struggled with and debated what exactly makes one a serial killer and if in fact one is truly born evil, or born to kill. For the family of the notorious South Carolina serial killer, Donald Henry "Peewee" Gaskins, the answer is simple.

"I think he was born to kill, I really do," was how Gaskins' daughter, Shirley, replied in an interview about her father.

But whether Gaskins was "born to kill" or if he was bred that way is for the most part a moot point to family members of the numerous people he killed in South Carolina during the 1960s and '70s. In the course of his career as a serial killer Gaskins is known to have murdered thirteen people who were unfortunate enough to cross his path, but he may have been responsible for over 100 murders, which, if true, would make him one of the most prolific serial killers in American history!

No one can doubt that Gaskins was dealt a bad hand in life: he was born to poverty, he never knew his biological father, and he was routinely beaten by his "uncles." Gaskins was also picked on by other kids as a child due to his diminutive stature. Because of his size, he only reached 5'4 as an adult, he earned the nickname "Peewee". One would think that with the nickname "Peewee" he was an easy going guy; but that person would be wrong . . . dead wrong!

Gaskins began his criminal career as a pre-teen by becoming involved in a street gang that pulled petty crimes before graduating to rape, burglary, aggravated assault, and eventually murder.

Today, Gaskins may not be as well-known as Jeffery Dahmer or Ted Bundy, but he was every bit just as scary as those two and in many ways more dangerous. Peewee was not a typical serial killer concerning his method of operation, pathology, and victimology: men, women, and children were all counted among his victims and he used a plethora of weapons to dispatch them.

He was also notable because his murders can be divided into two distinct categories – murders for pleasure and murders for profit. Donald Henry Gaskins was a man driven to kill – it was what he did and the one thing in life for which he truly had a talent. Because of his aptitude for murder he was able to make money killing and also use it as a twisted past-time.

Gaskins was also one of the first people to attain fame during his time for being a serial killer. Decades before websites dedicated to serial killers were even conceived, the news of Gaskins' deeds was replayed in newspapers and on television throughout the world. Gaskins became both famous and infamous. Eventually, the internet generation would learn of the Gaskins' deeds and have added him posthumously to many rogues galleries of killers.

The story of Donald Henry Gaskins is a cautionary tale that will bring those who follow it into the darkest recesses of human depravity. Gaskins was in many ways like your neighbor next door; but as will be revealed, nobody was safe when Gaskins was in the neighborhood.

Table of Contents

Chapter 1: A Killer Is Born or Bred? 1

    The Snake and the Rat 4

    Too Cool for School 6

    The Criminal Career Begins 7

    School Is in Session 11

    Peewee the Escape Artist 12

    Back in Florence County 14

Chapter 2: Peewee Finds His Power 17

    Becoming a "Powerman" 18

    In and Out 21

    The Tables Are Turned 21

    Peewee the Escape Artist: Part II 23

Chapter 3: A Monster Unleashed 25

    Killing for Pleasure 26

    The Coastal Killings 27

    Killing for Profit 30

    A Hired Gun 31

Chapter 4: Losing Control 34

Peewee's Hearse 35

Preying on Those Closest 35

Father and Daughter 38

Kim Ghelkins and the Capture of Gaskins 39

Chapter 5: The End of a Nightmare? 41

Even a Serial Killer Needs Friends 41

A Monster is Unearthed 45

Peewee Faces His Sins 47

A Reprieve 47

The Mounting Murders 49

Chapter 6: The Meanest Man in America 52

The Rudolph Tyner Murder Plot 52

Going Out with a Bang 56

Chapter 7: The End of the Road 59

Final Truth 61

One Last Kill? 63

A Familiar Companion 63

Chapter 8: A Serial Killer Outlier 66

    What is a Serial Killer? 66

    Peewee's Typology 67

    A Comparative Study 69

Chapter 9: The Legacy of Donald Henry Gaskins 73

Chapter 1:

A Killer Is Born or Bred?

In order to determine if Gaskins was born or became a serial killer, or a combination of the two took place, his youth must be considered. Gaskins was born on March 19, 1933 in Florence County, South Carolina to single mother and a life of poverty.

Donald's mother, Parrott, gave him his surname since it was not known who his father was. By all accounts Gaskin's mother gave him little else during his difficult childhood.

Adult supervision, in order to develop a moral compass or even for simple safety measures, was unknown to the young Gaskins. At the age of one, as he played in the family home unattended, Gaskins drank a bottle of kerosene that resulted in him having serious physical maladies for many years.

Gaskin's mother believed that the kerosene was the catalyst for her son's later problems. Richard Harpootlian, the man who successfully prosecuted Gaskins in the early 1980s, remains skeptical but leaves the door open as he said: "His mother thinks the kerosene drinking early on was the cause of his problems – I don't know."

The physical trauma caused by the kerosene was no doubt serious, but experts are not so quick to believe that it was the only, or even major, cause of Gaskins' depravity. Dr. Helen Morrison believes that it takes much more than serious physical trauma to create a serial killer. "If it were true that brain trauma had something to do with aggression then we would expect that every serial murderer would have some type of brain trauma or brain insult and that doesn't happen."

It will never be known how much, or little, of a role the kerosene drinking played in making Gaskins South Carolina's most prolific serial killer, but the effects lingered with him for several years. He suffered from convulsions until the age of three, was plagued by nightmares throughout his youth, and the chemical may have stunted his growth, which ultimately resulted in his short stature.

But the nightmare of his youth was all too real.

As his mother neglected him, her steady supply of lovers gave Gaskins plenty of attention in the form of regular, brutal beatings. His uncles would also join in for good measure by invoking severe forms of corporal punishment that were no doubt intended to satiate their devious desires more than to elicit positive responses from Gaskins.

"When I was younger there was always one or another of a bunch of different step-daddies around. I called them all sir and never bothered to learn most of their names because I knew my mama wasn't married to them, and they wouldn't likely be around for long," said Gaskins on his mother's lovers.

Eventually, Gaskins mother married one of her lovers, but instead of providing a sense of stability, Peewee's stepfather continued the cycle of physical abuse.

"The one she finally did marry was one mean son-of-a-bitch. He used to back-hand me and knock me clean across the room just for practice," noted Gaskins. "But then everybody knocked me around: my uncles, my other step-daddies."

About the only thing Gaskins got from his family was his nickname, but it was not given in a loving, or even joking manner, in fact, it was not "until I was a teenager and got sentenced to the reformatory" that Peewee learned his real name was "Donald."

The nickname stuck in more ways than one. "I never growed enough to keep up with others. That's how I got the nickname 'Peewee Peewee Peewee, playing with your Pee pee' they used to say, and when I got mad and hit somebody, that was all the excuse they needed to gang up and beat the hell out of me," said Gaskins on how his peers teased him.

It is interesting that a nickname as innocuous as "Peewee" came to represent one of the worst serial killers in American history. It was a nickname that emanated from hatred for Gaskins and he was more than happy to reciprocate those feelings towards the society as a whole.

But it was not just his tough upbringing or the torment of other children that pushed him in a violent direction. There was always something dark beneath the surface of Donald Henry Gaskins.

The Snake and the Rat

One of the more interesting anecdotes from Gaskins' youth that may indicate the direction he was headed involved a trip to a carnival.

Peewee, along with his mother and stepfather, went into a tent to view a collection of snakes with a large king cobra being the main attraction.

Something stirred in Gaskins.

"Then the barker stopped talking, took a live rat out of a box, and dropped it in the cage with the snake. The rat ran around and around real fast. The cobra stirred and coiled, rose up and flared out its neck, and the rat stopped, froze like it thought if it stayed still, it might turn invisible," said Peewee. "What took hold of my attention right then was that the cobra's head was almost exactly as high up as my head. When I looked through the glass I was staring it straight in the eye and my reflection looked like that cobra and me had the same head and face and eyes."

What happened next probably best encapsulates the life that Gaskins would later live. " 'Ladies and gentlemen,' the Barker started talking again: 'most animals either kill for food or to defend themselves. A cobra eats twice a week. This one was fed last night. That bulge halfway down its length is the supper it is still digesting. So let me assure you, this snake is not hungry. And as you no doubt noticed when you walked up to its cage the cobra didn't get upset. It just lays there. That's because it is used to people and knew it didn't need to defend itself. But now suddenly it has raised itself up and is about to strike – and that ladies and gentlemen, is what make the cobra the most dangerous of all reptiles – the fact that even as we watch it, it is preparing to kill for no reason other than the fact that it has decided to kill.' The snake struck, then stretched out and went back to sleep," noted Peewee. "The rat didn't move. I looked at my reflection, then at the cobra and I turned and saw my girl cousin holding tight to my mama's leg, and I looked up at my mama's and step-daddy's faces and saw that they seemed pretty scared, too." Gaskins continued, "I had a hard-on. And I knew that what I had just seen was somehow special and important, even though I didn't know why."

Peewee had found his spirit animal!

Too Cool for School

As Gaskins moved through his childhood he found the rigors of formal education to be especially restrictive. Most kids at least pass through a phase where they hate school, but for Peewee it was much more.

For Gaskins school became a place that he truly dreaded.

School was also another place where Peewee was abused. "To me, school was more than just a waste, it was a kind of torture. Everybody picked on me, so I got into fights almost every day, and then I got punished by the teachers and principal for fighting," noted Peewee. "It's no wonder I never learned jackshit . . . My step-daddy said if I weren't going to school I had to work in the fields and do more chores. I said I wanted to work on cars, not on a farm, but he beat my ass so hard every time I slipped off to work for the mechanic that I decided it was best just to do whatever he wanted."

But Gaskins' stepfather's concern was rooted more in a sense of power over his stepson than any real concern for his future. Peewee began to do whatever he wanted, but in order to avoid punishment from his stepfather he learned how to conceal his indiscretions better.

Eventually deception became another tool that Gaskins learned to utilize quite well. Gaskins discovered that if he could hide his truancy from his stepfather then there were also any number of things he could hide from him as well.

The young Gaskins was learning quickly the skills needed to become a criminal, which he would then use years later to become a serial killer.

The Criminal Career Begins

Finding no support at home and searching for acceptance elsewhere, Gaskins entered the criminal underworld at the tender age of eleven when he dropped out of school. Soon after leaving school, Gaskins teamed up with two other dropouts his age and formed a street gang called the "Trouble Trio" that terrorized Florence County with an assortment of petty crimes.

Gaskins and his young cohorts focused most of their criminal energies on burglary and gambling, but this is the period where the future serial killer would get his first taste of sexual sadism.

To Peewee's family and the authorities of South Carolina this should have been the first signs that they had a potential serial killer in their midst. As researcher Laurence Miller wrote: "Sexuality necessarily entails vulnerability, and that vulnerability can either be shared for the purposes of enhanced human intimacy, or exploited for the infliction of human cruelty and horror."

Throughout his life Gaskins chose to use sexuality to exploit and harm others.

The Trouble Trio used some of their ill-gotten gains to procure prostitutes and they also sexually assaulted a number of local boys. After the trio committed their assaults they then threatened to do worse if the boys told their parents or the authorities. The gang also turned their savage lust towards one of their own member's family.

The trio gang raped one of the member's sisters for which all three boys received beatings from their parents, but no official punishment from the courts. Peewee learned that intimidation works and the more he intimidated people the less likely they were to talk to the authorities. Florence County became his sadistic playground and as former sheriff William Barnes said: "They were all scared of him in the lower county."

Peewee's hatred of women was well documented and can be seen in the number of women he killed throughout his crime spree, but the feelings were manifested at an early age. The lack of support by Gaskins' mother no doubt contributed, but something much more was at work.

The attitude that Gaskins had towards women at an early age is best summarized in his own words. "Even back then, girls pissed me off," said Peewee. "It especially made me mad that them bitches could do anything they wanted – show their asses, make fun of me, even beat me up – and dare me to do anything about it, knowing I couldn't do nothing without being punished by grown-ups."

If Gaskins' family actually cared then perhaps they would have seen the signs of an early serial killer in their midst. Laurence Miller wrote: "A frequent association appears between serial homicide and two other crimes: burglary and rape." Miller continued: "While the reasons for this particular association are not settled, it seems evident that both of these crimes involve the willful violation of another person's intimate self, either their home or their physical body. Burglaries and rapes are, in essence, both *invasions* of another person who has been dehumanized."

Since Gaskins' family was unwilling to get him the help he needed then it was up to the authorities of Florence County to deal with the budding criminal.

Putting an end to Peewee's juvenile crime spree would not be easy for the authorities of Florence County, but they were aided by the bravery of one of Gaskins' victims.

After the gang rape incident, the other two members of the Trouble Trio moved out of the area, which left Peewee to continue to ravage the county alone. In 1946, at the age of thirteen, Gaskins met a victim who was willing to fight back!

As Gaskins was burglarizing a home, he was interrupted by a girl he knew who then proceeded to attack him with an axe. Peewee was able to wrest the axe from the girl, which he then used to attack her. Leaving the girl for dead, Gaskins then went about his burglary and left the scene believing that he successfully disposed of the only witness who could finger him. Gaskins failed to consider the strength of his victim.

The young girl, who suffered serious head wounds from the attack, managed to crawl to a nearby stream that kept her alive until she was found. Gaskins daughter, Shirley, stated that "that only thing that kept her alive was a little bit of water trinkling through there and it kept her alive until someone found her."

The young victim recovered from her wounds and was able to identify Gaskins as her attacker.

Gaskins was convicted of attempted murder and sentenced to reform school until his eighteenth birthday. But Peewee soon learned that the institution he was sent to did little to reform and the education he received was in predatory studies.

School Is in Session

Most thirteen year olds spend their time playing sports, hanging out with their friends, experimenting with love, and for the more ambitious, studying. But Donald Gaskins was not like most thirteen year olds as his time was spent being victimized and in turn learning how to be a better predator.

Almost immediately after Gaskins arrived at the South Carolina Industrial School for Boys he was beaten and gang-raped by several of the other inmates. His small stature was apparently what made him a target as his daughter Shirley said he was "a tiny, tiny person and you know, the bigger boys heaped on him."

One could argue that Gaskins was finally getting what he deserved and a more introspective, self-aware person may have seen things that way and so determined to travel on a new path; but Gaskins, like most serial killers, lacked self-awareness and empathy.

To survive in the juvenile facility Gaskins sexually serviced the strongest inmate in the cell block who was known as the "boss boy."

For the most part the boss boys protected Peewee from the sexual advances and violence from the other boys, but he also ended up with one who instigated a gang rape on Gaskins. Peewee said that this particular boy enjoyed to "watch gang-rapes with me on the bottom." Gaskins learned a lot in juvenile hall about human behavior and the criminal underworld, but he also learned it was a place he did not want to be.

Peewee also spent much of his four years escaping numerous times from the juvenile facility.

Peewee the Escape Artist

Besides his plethora of murders, Gaskins ability to escape from confinement became another one of the hallmarks of his criminal career. His slippery reputation began while he was in the juvenile facility when he ran to escape the sexual abuse from his fellow inmates and the cruelty of the guards.

After serving about a year in the juvenile hall, Gaskins and four other boys ran from the facility. The other boys were quickly captured, but Peewee managed to make it to one of his many hideouts in Florence County.

A police officer, who knew Gaskins and also knew that he was supposed to be in the juvenile hall, noticed Peewee lurking around an abandoned house. The cop convinced Peewee to return voluntarily to the reformatory.

Although Peewee returned the juvenile hall willingly, he was severely punished by the authorities.

For his efforts Gaskins was given thirty lashes and sentenced to a month of hard labor.

The experience only hardened Peewee's resolve more; but for his second escape attempt he changed his method of operation a bit by only having one partner.

Peewee was a bit more successful in his second attempt as he was able to elude the authorities for a week before they used bloodhounds to catch up with him in a wooded area.

From an early age Gaskins found the woods and swamps of South Carolina to be a sanctuary from the pressures of a world that he felt was constantly against him. Gaskins would continue to hide in these woods and swamps throughout his adult life whenever he either escaped from a correctional facility or was wanted for a crime.

The woods and forests that Peewee ran to as a child were also the same places that later served as the makeshift graveyards for his many victims,

After being captured for his second escape, Gaskins was severely beaten and given four months of hard labor.

Gaskins escaped twice more from juvenile custody. The third escape resulted in one of his family members informing authorities to his whereabouts and after the fourth escape he joined a traveling carnival.

While he was traveling with the carnival he met a thirteen year old girl who he would marry. Wives, like murder victims, were something that Peewee like to collect as he acquired six before his death.

Back in Florence County

When Gaskins was finally released in 1950 the authorities saw what kind of problem he posed to society. His release report stated that Gaskins was "anti-social and there is something in his past development that is praying upon his mind." The report further read: "We consider him dangerous and also believe that he has the homicidal tendencies peculiar to a paranoid type."

Peewee left the reformatory and returned to Florence County a better criminal and a more dangerous predator.

Gaskins quickly found work in the tobacco fields of South Carolina and just as quickly devised a couple of ways to profit criminally from his new job. In one scheme Peewee would steal tobacco from his employers and sell it on the open market, while he also later burned down barns in the age-old insurance scam. He would get paid a few dollars by farmers to burn down their barns and they would then collect the insurance money.

It is unknown the extent of the pleasure Gaskins derived from these arsons, but as will be seen later, Peewee mixed business and pleasure in many of his crimes. As a young man committing a string of arsons Gaskins fit the profile of a serial killer in training as Laurence Miller noted in a study that "these children often lie, steal, destroy property, set fires, and are cruel and callous to other kids." Arson also has a sexual component for many would be serial killers.

The young Gaskins displayed all the hallmarks of a potential serial killer with his lack of empathy, predilection for cruelty, and general anti-social attitude.

After only a year of freedom, Gaskins' inherent violence manifested itself once more towards a young woman. Peewee's victim was a tobacco farmer's daughter who had the misfortune to ask Gaskins why he was burning her father's barn and by some accounts, also laughed at him.

A combination of fear of arrest for the arsons and his deep seated hatred of women and love of violence drove Gaskins to attack the girl with a hammer. Luckily, the girl survived, which meant that Gaskins soon found himself in the tough adult men's prison in Columbia, South Carolina.

Chapter 2:

Peewee Finds His Power

After Gaskins was sentenced for the attempted murder of his boss' daughter, he found himself in a familiar environment – a correctional institution. He also found himself in a familiar situation as a potential victim.

Although Gaskins was a predator, up until this time he was the lowest rung on the criminal underworld totem pole and subject to the whims of stronger, more powerful inmates.

Most American prisons operate on a hierarchy where the bottom is filled with the weakest inmates, often sex offenders, while the most powerful inmates are the ones who display a combination of intelligence, physical strength, and a detached cruelty. Prison gangs are also very powerful organizations in American prisons and the state prison in Columbia, South Carolina during the 1950s was no different.

The state penitentiary in Columbia – today known as Central Correctional Institute in Columbia (CCI) – in 1952 was a depressing, violent, and overcrowded place. From 1930 to

1960 the population of the prison more than tripled from 687 inmates to 2,078, which added to the tension already inherent in such a place.

Peewee had his work cut out for him surviving in Columbia.

Becoming a "Powerman"

The top predator inmates in the Columbia prison during the 1950s were known as the "Powermen." The Powermen lived relatively easy lives behind bars as they were given the best job details by the authorities and they routinely extorted weaker inmates for commissary items and sexual favors. Peewee knew that if he could become a Powerman then his life behind bars would be one that he could tolerate and possibly excel at; Gaskins had a goal!

Not long after Gaskins arrived at the state prison he was threatened with violence and told that he would have perform sexual favors to prevent being killed. At this point in his life Gaskins had been both the victim and perpetrator of sexual violence and he had to make a decision: submit to the inmate's sexual advances and become his "bitch", or kill an inmate publicly in order to prove that he belongs at the top of the prison hierarchy.

Peewee chose a Powerman with a most unusual name for his victim – Hazel Brazell. By every account Brazell defied his feminine sounding first name as inmates and guards alike never used it. But killing Brazell would not be easy; all things being equal Peewee was no match for the larger Brazell in a fight, so Gaskins would resort to tactics that he employed countless times throughout his serial killer career – he would stalk his prey.

Gaskins would become the snake and Brazell was the rat!

Peewee spent a couple of weeks ingratiating himself to Brazell and gaining his confidence by bringing the Powerman food from the kitchen. Once Peewee saw that Brazell had sufficiently let his guard down he then decided it was time to act.

Gaskins took a paring knife stolen from the kitchen and calmly walked to Brazell's cell past other Powermen who let Peewee pass because his presence was by then a normal occurrence.

Once inside Brazell's cell, Peewee was relieved to find that the kill would be much easier then he originally thought as his mark was on the toilet. Not wasting anytime, Gaskins quickly attacked Brazell, cutting his throat and leaving him to bleed to death on the hard, cold floor of the Columbia penitentiary.

Peewee was quickly apprehended by the guards and subsequently charged with Brazell's murder in county court, but due to the latter's violent reputation and size Gaskins was able to plea bargain the charge down to manslaughter, most of which ran concurrent with the sentence he was already serving.

Peewee achieved his goal because not only did the other inmates leave him alone, but he was also initiated into the Powermen. "I wouldn't never again have to be afraid of anybody in the pen no matter how long I was there," said Gaskins.

The murder of Brazell was Gaskins' first confirmed kill, which seemed to have set the scene for the killing spree that was yet to come. Professor David Wilson believes that Gaskins' first kill was where he found his power as it was "the beginnings of Gaskins overcoming these childhood problems about his size and actually using the fact that he's small, but dangerous, to his advantage."

In the book *Final Truth*, Gaskins related how much better his life behind bars was after he established himself at the top of the prison food chain. "What I mean is that I could get pretty much anything I needed. I had the system working for me . . . I had power and my weapon and all the young meat I wanted."

In and Out

Gaskins spent most of the better part of the '50s and '60s in prison with most of the time he spent on the streets being "self-furloughs" he took in the form of escapes.

Unlike most of his earlier escapes from juvenile facilities, Gaskins' escapes from adult prisons were more successful as his periods of freedom were much longer.

In 1955, after Gaskins learned that his wife planned to divorce him, he escaped from the Columbia penitentiary through a garbage truck.

Peewee then stole a car and drove to Florida where he met up with the carnival he travelled with earlier in his life. Although he never caught up with his wife, he met another woman who he married (while still legally married to his first wife) and subsequently left after only two weeks.

The Tables Are Turned

Throughout Gaskins adult criminal career he was the consummate predator who was also in control, especially when it came to women. His hatred for women is well documented, which makes the events of his time on the lam in 1955 all that more interesting.

After Peewee left his wife of two weeks, he fled to Tennessee with a side show contortionist name Bettie Gates he met at the carnival. Gaskins was enamored and enthralled with the woman and apparently was also oblivious to her machinations.

After the duo arrived in Tennessee, Gates told Gaskins that she needed money to bail her brother out of jail. Gates gave Peewee a carton of cigarettes and some money to deliver to her brother, but when Gaskins returned to the hotel he was sharing with Gates he discovered that both her and their stolen car were gone.

Peewee had been duped – he was the rat and Gates was the snake!

To make matters worse, local police soon arrived at Gaskins' hotel room with the news that the carton of cigarettes he delivered to the jail concealed a weapon that Gates' brother used to escape.

Also, Gates' brother was actually her husband!

Eventually the police discovered that Peewee was a wanted fugitive and returned him to South Carolina to not only serve the remainder of his current sentence, but also to face new charges that stemmed from his escape.

Peewee the Escape Artist: Part II

Gaskins numerous escapes from correctional facilities, while he was a juvenile and adult, demonstrate that he was tenacious, patient, and had to ability to think in an organized manner. The escapes also show that Gaskins was no dummy. The numerous escapes that Peewee pulled were a chance for him to showcase some of his talents and also to learn some new ones.

While on the lam Peewee was able to enhance his criminal skills and he also learned how to live off the land.

Like many criminals in a similar situation, Gaskins often returned to his home after some of his escapes, but he had enough sense to avoid populated areas. Because he knew that few law enforcement officials would follow him there, Peewee learned how to live in the forests and swamps of Florence County, South Carolina. According to his daughter he survived by "eating snakes, he'd eat rattlesnake." For water he would "take water out of the ditches and stuff and boil it and drink it."

In one particular escape Gaskins leapt from a second story window in a courthouse and then fled to his familiar swampland. The authorities were hot on his heels with bloodhounds, but Peewee managed to outflank the police, circle back around, and wrote "Peewee Was Here" on the windshield of one of their cars.

During his periods of freedom, Gaskins also found plenty of time to perfect his criminal crafts. After he was paroled legitimately in 1961, Gaskins briefly worked as a driver and personal assistant for a traveling minister. But none of the preacher's sermons had a positive effect on Gaskins because he used the job as cover to burglarize homes throughout South Carolina.

Perhaps this is where Gaskins first learned that mobility is the key to avoiding detection. Although most of Peewee's murders took place in South Carolina, his coastal killings took place over a large area of the state and into North Carolina. He always stayed one step ahead of the authorities.

In 1962 Gaskins was convicted of the statutory rape of a twelve year old girl, which landed him in prison until 1968. When Peewee was released from prison he vowed never to return.

South Carolina was about to experience a murderous crime wave.

Chapter 3:

A Monster Unleashed

The period in Gaskins' life after his release from prison in 1968 can best be summed up as volatile, violent, and in some ways quintessentially that of a serial killer. Although Gaskins is officially attributed to thirteen murders, he may have killed eighty to ninety people. The high number would make him among the most prolific, if not the most prolific, of American serial killers. But equally disturbing and unique was his pathology and victimology.

Gaskins is a rarity among serial killers because he killed for both personal gain and pleasure. According to many accounts, he was driven by an insatiable urge to make others suffer, but he also supported himself financially through criminal endeavors – sometimes the motives would overlap.

The type of victims Gaskins chose also did not conform to any standard profile of serial killer victimology. Concerning the victims of serial killers, Laurence Miller wrote: "The victims of serial murder are predominantly female, white, and young adults, although same-sex murders are not uncommon, and some serial killers target children."

What is amazing and perhaps the most frightening aspect of Gaskins victims' profiles is that he killed in every one of the above categories. Peewee killed young and old, male and female, and for pleasure and profit. And although his victims were overwhelming white – interracial killing is most common among serial killers – in his final tally he counted two black and one mixed race victim.

Killing for Pleasure

US Highway 17 is a major four lane highway that connects the coastal cities of Wilmington, North Carolina near its northern end, to the South Carolina cities of Myrtle Beach and Charleston.

US 17, which runs parallel to the intracoastal waterway, sees thousands of vacationers drive over its asphalt daily as they head to the beach for some sun and fun.

The Carolina coasts were especially popular during the late 1960s and early '70s with young people as countless hitch hikers, hippies, and other assorted "drop outs" came there from all over the country. For the vast majority of those who came to coastal Carolina during the '60s and '70s their intentions were innocent and amounted to a desire to have some fun in the sun and possibly get a tan.

But Peewee did not come to the beach for a tan, he came to kill.

The Coastal Killings

It is believed that Gaskins found his first coastal victim in 1969 near Myrtle Beach, South Carolina. Urged by strong sadist urges, Peewee picked up an attractive female hitchhiker and propositioned her for sex. When the young woman spurned Gaskins' advances he beat her unconscious and then raped and tortured her before ending her life. Gaskins then took the body to the swamps he knew so well and sank it to the bottom.

After Peewee picked up his first coastal victim he was faced with a murderous revelation; he could do whatever he wanted to this person. "And the answer was simple: what I had to do was kill her. I remember smiling to myself and wondering why I hadn't ever thought of that before? If she was dead, she couldn't tell the law or nobody nothing – so once I had made up my mind and decided that she was going to die anyhow, I could do anything I wanted with her," said Gaskins.

And what Peewee did to this poor young woman and his other coastal victims is truly horrifying.

"Some of them I cut. Some I burned. I ran a cable in and out one, and hung her up by it. I pumped another one full of water, which seemed to really hurt, filling her up until it came out of her nose and mouth, but she died quick, which I hadn't expected, so I didn't do that anymore. I preferred for them to last as long as possible," said Gaskins about his coastal killings.

Peewee found inspiration for his torture methods by shopping in hardware stores. As he browsed through the hammers, saws, icepicks, and other tools that most people use for home repair, Gaskins' mind was fixated on torture and murder.

Gaskins claims that he took as many as eighty victims, both female and male, during his string of coastal killings.

In 1974 Peewee picked up two hitchhikers that he thought were women from behind because of their long hair, but as the two got into his car he realized they were long haired young men.

Unfortunately for the two young men Gaskins did not discriminate when it came to murder victims. He raped and tortured both men before cannibalizing parts of their bodies and then disposing of them in a swamp.

The method of killing that Gaskins followed during his coastal killings, which was usually preceded by lengthy torture sessions, fits the profile of a sexually sadistic serial killer. But Gaskins took his sadism a step further.

Peewee claims that as he cannibalized a number of his coastal victims he often forced them to watch as he ate bits of their flesh and even made some of his victims eat parts of their own bodies!

For most people it is a futile attempt to try to understand what drove Gaskins to not only kill, but especially the manner in which he did. Perhaps the deviancy can best be described in the words of Gaskins himself as he once told his daughter that "he would get this urge that he would have to see blood. He called himself a vampire."

Throughout the '60's and '70s Peewee may have killed as many as ten to twelve people a year along the coastal highways of North and South Carolina. As his murder spree continued, the urge to "see blood" that his daughter described grew exponentially. Dr. Helen Morrison relates that increased frequency of killings was an obsession that grew into an addiction. "It's a little scary to say that a serial murderer is an addict; but if you really look at it in that context, in a way they are an addict, they have to do it."

As Peewee's homicidal addiction grew he found new ways to satiate himself and make money at the same time. Gaskins moved into the next phase of his serial killer career.

"By October of seventy, I had picked up and coastal killed ten girls, total, including the three done in sixty-nine. But the most important thing about nineteen-and-seventy was that it was the year I started doing my Serious Murders," reminisced Gaskins.

Gaskins would claim to continue his coastal killings for weekend recreation, but most of his energies became focused on killing for profit and those closest to him.

Killing for Profit

To Donald Henry Gaskins killing was a past time, but it was also much more than that – it was his vocation!

Many of Gaskins' victims and most of his thirteen confirmed kills were men and women he killed for some sort of monetary profit. He killed people in the process of robberies, some as part of contract assassinations, and others who he believed would snitch him out to the authorities and send him back to prison. If Peewee thought that he could gain financially from a murder he would most likely do it.

Twenty five year old Dennis Bellamy and his fifteen year old half-brother, Johnny Knight, made the short-sighted decision of becoming involved with Gaskins in an auto theft ring.

Gaskins arranged to meet Bellamy and Knight in a wooded area near his home in order to discuss the future of their criminal alliance. Apparently Peewee was worried that one, or both, of the men were talking to authorities about their activities. When the two arrived at Peewee's home he led them into the woods near his home in rural Florence County, South Carolina. It would be the last walk the two men took.

According to sheriff William Barnes, after walking some distance in the woods Gaskins pointed up to a particularly high tree limb and commented that they could use it to hoist stolen vehicles. When the men looked at the limb "he shot one of them in the back of the head and then when the other one ran he shot him."

Gaskins then disposed of the two bodies in a communal burial site he created.

The exact reason why Gaskins killed Bellamy and Knight is unknown but Shirley Gaskins stated that her father would kill any business associates he felt were a threat: "If he thinked they were gonna, you know, they were getting tired or they were gonna tell on him then he'd get rid of em."

A Hired Gun

By 1975 Peewee had killed scores of people, for both pleasure and profit, so he decided to put his homicidal skills on the free market. Gaskins was approached by a woman named Suzanne Kipper to kill her ex-boyfriend, Silas Yates, for $1,500.

As a local of Florence County, Kipper was well acquainted with Gaskins' reputation for acts of extreme violence and so believed that Peewee was the man for the job.

Kipper was right in her assessment of Gaskins' homicidal abilities, but ultimately Yates was not the only victim in the murder conspiracy.

Gaskins, along with three accomplices named Diane Neely, John Powel and John Owens, plotted and carried out the murder. Because Peewee's violent reputation preceded him in the county, Neely, Powel, and Owens had to lure Yates from the safety of his home. Once outside, where Gaskins was lurking, Yates was helpless as Peewee then pounced on his hapless victim.

After Peewee killed Yates, the other three helped him dispose of the body and all conspirators left happy, until Gaskins received the phone call.

Not long after the Yates murder Diane Neely and her boyfriend, Avery Howard, contacted Gaskins and threatened to turn him in to the authorities unless he paid the two $5000.

Peewee feigned compliance with the extortion scheme and agreed to pay money.

Apparently Neely and Howard either underestimated Gaskins' killing prowess or they believed he was too dumb to know that they would implicate themselves in the murder, or both, because they agreed to meet Peewee in a neutral location to receive the payoff.

Neely and Howard were never heard from again.

The two criminals were added to Gaskins' growing body count in the woods and swamps of Florence County, South Carolina.

The murders of Neely and Howard were two of the last that Gaskins would commit as a free man, but before he was arrested he committed some of his most heinous murders.

Chapter 4:

Losing Control

For most of his serial killer career Gaskins was able to compartmentalize his killings into two categories: "weekend recreation" was what he called the coastal killings, while "serious killings" are what he termed the murders for profit. Serious killings are also what he called the murders he committed on those closest personally to him.

Until the early 1970s Peewee was able to separate the two categories somewhat effectively, which no doubt delayed his capture; but things began to change when friends, acquaintances, and family members of Donald Henry Gaskins began to disappear.

Gaskins could longer control and compartmentalize his homicidal urges. Anyone who came into contact with him was a potential victim.

Peewee's Hearse

As Gaskins killing spree progressed into the mid '70s Peewee seemed to become more brazen. He began to do things that pointed out not only his eccentricities, but quite possibly his thinly veiled life as a serial killer.

Perhaps he felt that since he had already killed several people and was never even a suspect that he would never get caught, no matter how outlandish his behavior was.

Peewee began driving a hearse that had inscribed on it "I hold dead bodies", as if to throw it in the community's face what he was doing. Despite this, people just saw him as a strange, eccentric character, as Sheriff Barnes noted: "I think you would have to say that he came over as different because how many people do you know that drive a hearse for their vehicle?"

It was around this time that Peewee also became more brazen concerning his victims.

Preying on Those Closest

Most notorious serial killers in history were able to separate their vocation of killing from their personal lives. Some, such as Ted Bundy and Gary Ridgeway, were even able to conduct personal relationships with numerous people who had no idea of their devious and diabolical crimes. Gaskins was also able to maintain a similar façade for a number of years, but eventually everything began to unravel.

Although Peewee's violent and criminal reputation preceded him in Florence County, most of the residents thought of him more as an oddball and few if any suspected that he was South Carolina's most notorious serial killer, because he was careful.

Gaskins coastal victims were people he had no connection with, while the victims of his profit killings were usually criminals and drifters that few people missed. Despite being two very different victimologies, they were actually well compartmentalized and kept the authorities well off his track.

But all of that would change in 1970 when Peewee could no longer restrain his murderous impulses. This is when the string of murders he termed "serious murders" began.

Beginning in 1970 Gaskins began killing acquaintances, friends, and even family members who were unfortunate enough to ask him for a favor or even stop by the house for a visit.

In November, 1970 Gaskins saw his fifteen year old niece, Janice Kirby, and her friend Patricia Alsobrook walking home so he did as any family would do and offered them a ride.

But Peewee had evil plans as he brought the two girls to an abandoned house where he raped, tortured, and eventually drowned both to death.

Around this same time Gaskins also preyed on another family friend who fell victim to Peewee's helpful façade.

Twenty three year old Doreen Dempsey planned to leave the state with her two year old child in order to start over. Dempsey was a single mother and her child was racially mixed so she believed that there would be better opportunities for both of them outside of rural South Carolina. After Dempsey packed her and her child's belongings into a couple of suitcases they were ready to catch a bus out of town. Since she did not own a car and the rural area had no cab service, she needed a ride from a friend.

Gaskins offered to drive Dempsey and her child to the bus station, but neither ever arrived.

Gaskins instead drove the two to one of his swampy graveyards where he raped and killed Doreen before turning his unnatural fury on the child. "He said he could not resist raping the baby," is what Shirley Gaskins said concerning the murders.

It was also during his string of acquaintance murders that Peewee claimed his first black victim. Martha Dicks was a twenty year old black woman who ran in some of the same circles as Gaskins and could often be seen hanging around his repair shop. Although Peewee was known to be racist, he tolerated Dicks for some reason and even put up with some of her teasing.

But apparently Martha Dicks' jokes went too far.

For reasons unknown, in early 1971, Dicks began telling people that she was pregnant with Peewee's child.

Apparently that was too much for Gaskins so he once more laid a trap becoming the snake, while his victim was the rat.

He invited Dicks over to his shop one night for drinks that were laced with a fatal amount of sedatives. After she died, Gaskins dumped her body in a ditch and then went about his business.

In the end Dicks' murder was not for pleasure or profit, but according to Gaskins was due to her "lying mouth."

Father and Daughter

Perhaps one of the most bizarre aspects of Gaskins' acquaintance murders is the role that his daughter Shirley played in many of them. A number of Peewee's victims were cousins and playmates of his daughter, which indicates that the serial killer consciously used his daughter for bait.

Ever the consummate predator, Gaskins was always looking for another weapon in his arsenal and apparently his own daughter became an unwitting pawn in his sick game.

According to Shirley he would often bring his victims by the house where she would make their last meal after which "they would leave and never come back."

Kim Ghelkins and the Capture of Gaskins

Perhaps feeling untouchable, Gaskins continued to focus his homicidal urges on people close to him. The last of his unfortunate victims in the string of "serious murders" was thirteen year old Florence County girl Kim Ghelkins.

Ghelkins had the audacity to rebuff one of Peewee's crude sexual advances. To rectify the insult Gaskins promptly abducted, raped, and murdered the girl and then placed her remains in the swampy graveyard whose vacancy was quickly filling.

But Kim Ghelkins was the wrong victim because there were people who missed her.

As the investigation into Ghelkins' disappearance commenced Donald Gaskins name kept surfacing. Could the strange ex-convict be responsible for the young girl's disappearance? Could he be responsible for more?

Evidence began to mount against Peewee and eventually the police obtained a search warrant for Gaskins' home that revealed clothing that belonged to Ghelkins. Peewee was arrested for contributing to the delinquency of a minor, but the seasoned career criminal would keep his mouth shut.

The evidence that got Peewee arrested initially for Ghelkins' disappearance was an item of clothing that could be definitively identified by her family members. Many serial killers take "trophies" or mementos from their victims, but Gaskins was not particularly fond of nostalgia, which is what makes the situation even more interesting.

In Gaskins own words he "made another mistake and didn't abide by the wise man's rule to never keep anything from a victim because it's evidence."

The clothing was enough to hold him in jail, but alone it was nowhere near enough evidence to get a murder conviction. For that the prosecutors would be fortunate enough to exploit another mistake Gaskins made.

Ultimately, Peewee's legal demise came as the result of something he chose to have that most people take for granted – a close friend and a confidant.

Chapter 5:

The End of a Nightmare?

For the people of Florence County, South Carolina the reign of terror imposed on them by Donald Henry Gaskins would end in 1975 when he was arrested in connection with Kim Ghelkins' murder. But Peewee's arrest proved to be just another chapter in the life of South Carolina's most prolific serial killer.

Historically, most serial killers work alone and the ones who operate in pairs, or even groups, do so in a manner that pits the killers against the rest of the world. Serial killers rarely confide their deeds until after they are caught, which is another aspect of Donald Henry Gaskins' serial killer career that makes him unique.

Even a Serial Killer Needs Friends

In tracing Donald Gaskins' criminal career it becomes apparent fairly quickly, due to his body count, that he had no use for friends and even less for "work place" acquaintances. Gaskins was good at keeping his homicidal secrets until he met Walter Neely.

Walter Neely was a criminal acquaintance of Gaskins' from Florence County who shared some of the same anti-social tendencies with the serial killer, although the two were never very close until 1975.

As Gaskins' killing frenzy reached its apex in 1975, Peewee became unhinged and made more and more mistakes. One night as he trolled the highways of South Carolina with nefarious purposes his heart raced as he spotted a possible mark – a van broken down on the side of the road.

Posing as a concerned citizen, Gaskins surveyed the situation and then quickly dispatched of the three victims, two females and a male, who were unfortunate enough to have broken down in Peewee's territory.

But this was not a typical Gaskins murder. It was much more impulsive, disorganized, and involved multiple victims. Peewee tortured and handcuffed the three before drowning them in a swamp. The three pleaded for their lives to no avail as Gaskins sent them all to their slow, watery doom. "It's hard to say which one suffered the most. I tried to make it equal," said Gaskins about the triple homicide.

As Peewee watched his victims sink into their watery graves he felt the familiar combination of thrill and relief that he had felt from his numerous other murders; but it was soon replaced with fear.

Peewee knew he needed help to clean up his mess.

"I had a real serious problem on my hands: the van," Gaskins said. "It was sure to get found, which was sure to bring the law, who was sure to ask questions all up and down the highway."

As stated earlier, Gaskins was avoided by most in Florence County and feared by many as his bizarre and sometimes violent reputation preceded him. Despite this, Gaskins was an accomplished criminal, which meant that he was able to collect a number of connections from his decades in the criminal underworld. One of these connections, which proved to be Gaskins' ultimate demise, was a man named Walter Neely.

Like Gaskins, Walter Neely was a local criminal who lived on the margins of polite society in Florence County, South Carolina. Neely was by no means a criminal mastermind and by most accounts was neither very bright nor particularly violent. But on the night that Peewee killed the three motorists, Neely was the man he called for help.

Neely drove the victim's van to Peewee's garage where the serial killer then used his mechanic skills to repaint and refurbish the vehicle in order to conceal it and profit from the murders. He then began to tell Neely everything.

Peewee's recital of his roster of murders had little to do with the quest for a catharsis and more with a twisted sense of pride. Gaskins had worked alone up to this point and aside from a couple of contract murders, most knew little about his predilection and aptitude for murder.

Gaskins began to let his guard down as he confided in Neely. Peewee showed his friend the dumpsites and Neely in turn even helped him dispose of more victims. One night Neely helped Gaskins kill two people who were dumb enough to steal from Peewee; later Peewee revealed even as he and Neely dumped the two bodies in one of his watery gravesites.

Eventually though Neely's friendship would be Gaskins' legal undoing.

As local, county, and state police began to focus on Gaskins for the Kim Ghelkins disappearance, they attempted to rattle all of the serial killer's friends and associates.

Walter Neely soon broke.

According to William Barnes: "After a lot of talking and everything Walter finally took the investigators out and showed them where he helped Peewee bury someone."

Neely brought investigators to dump site where Barnes said "they knew someone was buried there but we didn't know what we'd find until we started digging."

Admittedly, Gaskins broke his own code by confiding in Neely. Peewee said that if he had followed what he learned in prison from the other Powermen then he never would have been caught. "The time I spent with them was my college education," he wrote. "Since then, every time I have been faced with a problem or a choice I have thought back to the things that they said to me – and whenever I followed their advice, I always came out okay. It was the times I didn't do what they advised that I found myself in deep shit."

A Monster is Unearthed

When Walter Neely led investigators to one of Donald Henry Gaskins' dumpsites in rural South Carolina they did not know what they would find. Most were just hoping to find the body of Kim Ghelkins in order to give her a proper burial and her family closure, but they would be surprised and horrified with the level of depravity they unearthed.

Ira Parnell Jr. – who was a state investigator that worked on the Gaskins case and was there when Neely led authorities to the dumpsite – explained how he and about fifteen other law enforcement officers uncovered the site. "We just lined up and started walking slowly into the woods . . . sometime during that process in moving through the bushes and undergrowth somebody discovered that there were some bushes that had been put there, that weren't growing there," said Parnell.

It turned out to be the first of six bodies discovered at the site. Even seasoned law enforcement officers like Barnes had a difficult time grasping the scope of their discovery: "Yea it was a pretty gruesome scene . . . I guess I was overwhelmed. I had been in law enforcement for some twelve and a half years prior to this and I'd never seen anything of that magnitude."

The dumpsite was soon turned into an archaeological excavation as the investigators compiled a team to dig up and identify the bodies. The smell of death permeated the area. "I've never been a smoker, but the smell of decaying flesh was so intense in that area that, ah, the smoke from the cigars diminished that smell enough to where you could stand it," said Parnell.

All of the six bodies were buried in pairs. The first pair discovered was that of Bellamy and Knight who were among the victims of Gaskins' "profit" murders.

Peewee Faces His Sins

With the discovery of one of his dumping sites and his one friend cooperating with the authorities, the case against Donald Henry Gaskins was airtight. Both Gaskins and Neely were charged with eight counts of murder in Florence County, South Carolina on April 27, 1976.

Because the mountain of eye witness, circumstantial, and forensic evidence was uncontestable and insurmountable, Peewee was quickly convicted for the murder of Dennis Bellamy on May 24, 1976.

Appropriately, Gaskins was given the death sentence.

A Reprieve

After Gaskins was convicted of the Bellamy murder and sentenced to death, he quickly set about to manipulate the system. Like many career criminals, Peewee learned how to use laws and legal nuances to his advantage and so confessed to seven more murders under the agreement that he would not face the death penalty.

But Gaskins was sentenced to die for the Bellamy murder. Pleading guilty to avoid the death penalty in other murders seemed like a futile task; but Peewee would do everything in his power to give himself one more chance.

First the state would have to kill Peewee and in November, 1976 fate stepped in and gave Gaskins a reprieve when the U.S. Supreme Court ruled that the death penalty was unconstitutional.

Specifically, the Court ruled under *Woodson v. North Carolina* that states were forbidden to impose a mandatory death penalty as to do so would be a violation of the Eighth Amendment of the U.S. Constitution.

The ruling not only saved Gaskins' life, but it helped make him a celebrity in the South Carolina prison system.

Gaskins seemed to have a new lease on life after his death penalty was commuted to a life sentence. He was the cock of the walk behind bars as other inmates and even the guards were afraid to cross the notorious serial killer. As bad as life in prison would be for most normal people, Gaskins thrived in such an environment. He was truly at home in prison!

Gaskins reprieve was short lived though as in 1978 the United States Supreme Court overruled its original decision that banned capital punishment. The new ruling allowed for each state to pursue its own death penalty policies with South Carolina being quick to resume the practice.

The new situation put Peewee in a pickle: could Gaskins face the death penalty for the plethora of other murders he committed?

The Mounting Murders

Gaskins knew the clock was ticking so he set out once more to manipulate the system to his favor. His strategy was to confess to as many murders as he could whereby through a number of plea bargains he would avoid the death penalty for helping authorities clear the unsolved murders.

As Gaskins continued to work with authorities to clear unsolved murders, some law enforcement officers became skeptical of the sheer numbers that Peewee claimed to have killed. Despite the doubt, today experts point out that Gaskins had the ability and the means to carry out that many murders. "Could he have killed a hundred people? Sure he could have, um, but he would an outlier, that's a very high number of victims even for a prolific serial killer," said Professor David Wilson.

But after all Gaskins was a serial killer outlier in more ways than one!

One of Gaskins' more notable disputed confessions was of the abduction and murder of thirteen year old Margaret Cuttino in 1970. Peewee's confession to Cuttino's murder became particularly newsworthy because her father, James

Cuttino Jr., was a state senator. Also, by the time Gaskins confessed to killing Cuttino, another man, William Pierce, had already been convicted and sentenced to life in prison for her murder.

The details of Cuttino's murder are eerily similar to those of some of Gaskins' other victims during this same period. Cuttino was abducted in rural Sumter County, South Carolina on December 18 or 19, 1970 and her mutilated body was discovered on a dirt road nearly two weeks later on December 30.

Peewee was known to be in the area at the time.

After Gaskins' confession to her murder and the revelation of new evidence, many believed that Pierce would be exonerated or given a new trial; but South Carolina authorities remained adamant that Pierce, not Gaskins, was Cuttino's killer. Any chance of testing extant biological evidence from the crime scene for DNA was gone when authorities claimed Hurricane Hugo destroyed in the evidence in 1989.

In the book *Final Truth*, Gaskins expressed his frustration with the Cuttino case: "I admitted I killed Peggy, but I was ignored by the court because they already had Pierce doing life for killing her. I confessed because I knowed Junior Pierce weren't guilty and I didn't want him to end up in South Carolina's CCI for a crime he didn't commit."

But it would not be Gaskins' confession to Cuttino's or any other of his murders from the '60s and '70s that proved to be his final demise. It was behind bars that Peewee's greed and lust for murder finally became his downfall.

Chapter 6:

The Meanest Man in America

Although Donald Henry Gaskins may have killed up to 100 people before he landed in prison in the mid '70s, he earned his moniker "The Meanest Man in America" while serving his life sentence for the Bellamy murder.

Gaskins liked to do two things: kill people and commit crimes and he was not about to let the walls of a maximum security prison stop him from doing either one of those!

In 1982 Gaskins carried out the contract killing of a death row inmate that is seen by most people, even those who despise Peewee, as particularly daring and difficult, especially since Gaskins was not on death row!

The Rudolph Tyner Murder Plot

Gaskins' mark was a man named Rudolph Tyner who was described by prosecutor Richard Harpootlian as a "semi-retarded, very low IQ guy."

What placed the dimwitted Tyner in Gaskins' crosshairs was the double murder the former committed that landed him on South Carolina's death row. Tyner was convicted in 1978 for murdering an elderly couple named William and Myrtle Moon. The Moons owned and operated a small convenience store that was robbed by Tyner and according to court records, after the robbery he returned to ruthlessly execute the couple.

Although Tyner's conviction was air-tight and his execution was impending, not everyone was happy that the murderer continued to breathe.

The murdered couple's adopted son, Tony Cimo, became frustrated with the appeals process that kept Tyner alive and safe on death row so he decided to reach out to someone that could solve his problem – Donald Henry Gaskins.

"Tony was friends with someone in prison and they got daddy and Tony together," said Shirley Gaskins.

The intermediary was a career criminal from his home town named Jack Martin. Once Cimo contacted Martin about the plan, Peewee Gaskins was the first person that he recommended for the job.

Cimo apparently reached out at the right time to Gaskins, who was depressed about being unable to escape and needed something to release his pent up aggression. Tyner ended up being in the right place at the wrong time. "Because all this happened at the time I just described, when I wasn't making no headway with my own escape plans and was feeling even downer than usual, I took it as a personal challenge. Beside: I figured there weren't nobody in CCI I couldn't get to if I wanted, and it seems to me this Tyner truly did deserve to die," said Gaskins about Tyner.

Perhaps it is a bit of the pot calling or the kettle black when Gaskins said Tyner deserved to die, but once the plan was in motion Tyner's fate was sealed.

The relationship and situation that developed between Cimo and Gaskins proved to be so bizarre and unbelievable, but sometimes reality is stranger than fiction. In fact, the Tyner murder plot was so strange that it spawned a made for TV movie!

Although Gaskins truly enjoyed killing, his primary interest in the Tyner murder for hire plot was financial. He could care less about the lives of Cimo's parents or how they were murdered; in another time and under other circumstances Gaskins may have been their killer. This was another murder for profit, but the fact that Tyner was black also gave the openly racist Gaskins another reason to take his life.

Ultimately, the murder of Rudolph Tyner was more of a challenge than anything to the serial killer, as stated in his own words. The challenge was in two parts and involved: committing the murder in the first place and more importantly, getting away with it.

Through the prison contact, Cimo and Gaskins began formulating the plot to murder Tyner via phone calls that Peewee recorded with a tape deck recorder. Perhaps Gaskins feared that Cimo would try to blackmail him, or maybe Peewee planned to blackmail Cimo with the damning phone calls.

"Gerald wanted me to call you, said to tell you this is the doctor calling you," was what Gaskins said in the coded introductory call to Cimo.

As a doctor Gaskins' specialty was death and soon after the conversation with Cimo he went to work on Tyner.

Gaskins' murder of Tyner was not impulsive like many of his murders on the outside; in order to kill Tyner he had to get close and get his victim's confidence.

Peewee would kill Tyner in a similar fashion as he did to Brazell several years earlier in the same prison.

Peewee would once more become the snake, but this time Tyner was the rat.

One of the privileges that Peewee enjoyed in prison was greater freedom. He was allowed to roam more freely throughout the prison and from cell block to cell block, which is how he was able to befriend Tyner who was housed in the solitary confinement block of death row.

Gaskins would bring Tyner extra food and drugs such as marijuana from time to time. But Peewee was not being friendly or helpful, he was preparing his kill.

Peewee decided that this time he would use poison to dispatch his victim.

"We gave that son of a bitch all of it but one dose and all its doing is making that son of a bitch sick," said Gaskins to Cimo in a recorded status report about the murder plot. Unfazed, Gaskins attempted to poison Tyner again, this time with potential collateral damage present. "We'd put it in some damn buck for him to drink the other night and he drank and two more drank and all it was made all three of them sick as hell," said Gaskins to Cimo.

Poison was not working so Gaskins had to step up his game!

Going Out with a Bang

Gaskins knew that any more poison attempts on Tyner may reveal the murder plot so he formulated a new plan that became the stuff of legends.

One of the perks that Gaskins enjoyed in prison was being an inmate maintenance man. The job allowed him to roam freely throughout the prison, but more importantly, he was given a large supply of tools that he was allowed to keep in his cell. The tool set became the arsenal Peewee needed to carry out his final murder.

Gaskins was also allowed to move into the cell next to Tyner, which allowed him put the final part of his plan into action.

Peewee devised a jailhouse telephone that ran between his and Tyner's cell, which was intended to not only allow the two men to communicate with each other while they were locked in their cells, but also for Gaskins to finally kill his mark.

"I came up with something, he can't be no dam making sick on it. I need one electric cap and as much of a stick of damned dynamite as you can get," said Peewee to Cimo.

Yes, Peewee planned to blow up Tyner!

Although Cimo was not able to get dynamite to Gaskins, he was able to get the serial killer a small amount of C-4 plastic explosives. Once Peewee received the C-4 he transported it through the prison in secret compartment he cut into the heel of one of his work boots.

Gaskins then took a state issued drinking cup and sealed the blasting cap, explosives, and wires into it and gave it to Tyner with the explanation that it was his receiver for their jailhouse phone. Gaskins explained the process to Cimo: "I'll take a damned radio and rig it into a bomb and when he plugs that son of a bitch up, it will blow him into hell."

Peewee's technical expertise proved fatal because when Tyner put his receiver up to his ear the bomb went off killing him instantly.

"Pieces of him were blown all over the prison, fingers were everywhere," commented Harpootlian on the prison bombing.

The snake had struck, the rat was dead!

The tapes that Gaskins planned to possibly use against Cimo were discovered by prison authorities and used against both men in subsequent criminal proceedings.

Tony Cimo served six months of an eight year prison sentence for his role in the murder plot. The convoluted conspiracy eventually caught the eye of Hollywood as it provided the plot for a 1986 made for TV movie, *Vengeance: The Story of Tony Cimo*.

But for Gaskins the Tyner murder proved to be his final demise.

Chapter 7:

The End of the Road

After prison authorities learned of the complexity of Tyner's murder they turned the case over to the county prosecutor's office who promptly charged Gaskins with capital murder.

"The only good thing about that was, was that, you know, that was a crime that he could get the death penalty for," said William Barnes on the Tyner murder.

While awaiting trial Peewee began to finally get the attention that he so desperately sought. People from around the world were intrigued by the amazing murder he pulled off behind bars and they were equally horrified by the string of murders he committed before it.

Since it was a capital case, South Carolina law required that Gaskins be given two attorneys and since Peewee was indigent, he was given two court appointed lawyers – John Young and Jack Swerling.

A court appointed attorney does not imply that the lawyer, or in this case lawyers, are inferior, but just that the state will pay the lawyers' salaries for the duration of the case. Gaskins was lucky enough to get two of the best, high-profile criminal defense lawyers from the state of South Carolina because he would need all the help he could get.

But Peewee proved to be a difficult client as he tried to run the defense his own way.

Young said that when he first met Peewee in the prison visiting room he "told them to take the handcuffs off," which garnered the response, "You's aint afraid of Peewee?" from Gaskins.

Eventually, Young earned a certain level of respect from Peewee who told him: "I hate all lawyers except you."

But sometimes respect is a one way street. The more that Young worked with Gaskins the more he realized how utterly depraved and evil the man was. "He was the most evil human being – if you could call him human – that I've ever known," said Young.

While Gaskins' lawyers were working arduously on the lost cause of his defense, Peewee tried to generate his own alibi.

Gaskins wrote a couple letters to a friend named J.B. Brown asking him to admit to Tyner's murder to a priest named Frankie San. Peewee believed that once Brown "admitted" the murder to San, then the priest would have to tell the authorities, while not revealing his source due to priest privilege.

Peewee's plan was foiled when Brown went to the authorities and subsequently became one of the prosecution's star witnesses against Gaskins. There was nothing else Peewee could do but rely on his lawyers.

Young and Swerling did more than an admirable job, but the mountain of evidence against their client proved to be insurmountable.

In 1983 a South Carolina jury agreed that the evidence was overwhelming and so voted to convict Gaskins of capital murder. Shortly after his conviction the jury then came to another decision – that no one else should be the next victim of Donald Henry Gaskins, in prison or out, and so sentenced Peewee to death in the electric chair.

Final Truth

When Gaskins was sentenced to death he knew that it would be quite a few years before the state carried out the sentence. But with his freedoms severely curtailed Gaskins was forced to find new ways to kill time.

Gaskins would become famous!

While on death row Gaskins began to work with author Wilton Earl on the book *Final Truth: The Autobiography of Mass Murderer/Serial Killer Donald "Pee Wee" Gaskins*, which tells the story of Peewee's multi decade killing spree.

Earl communicated with Gaskins, through phone calls and visits, for over fifteen years to compile the book and give it a professional polish; but the gory details were all provided by Gaskins, quite willingly.

Peewee indicated that he was comfortable telling Earl his story, but that it would only be published *after* South Carolina executed him. "I never let anybody know what I've told her mainly because I couldn't let these things get knowed while I was alive and still fighting in court to keep out of the chair," Gaskins said. "And I never trusted no writer before not to publish until after I was dead."

When Gaskins was not working with Earl on the book he spent most of his time heavily medicated on death row. The isolation did not appeal to Peewee's freedom loving nature, but the drugs he received did: "The onliest good thing that come out of me being in isolated solitary was that the prison doctors started giving me heavier does of tranquilizers and sleeping pills, which they have kept on giving me, and which I have appreciated."

As the 1990s approached all of Gaskins' appeals were exhausted and no matter how famous he had become, he would never become a *cause celeb*. His date with destiny was fast approaching.

But Peewee would try to carry out one last major crime.

One Last Kill?

If the state of South Carolina thought that tranquilizers and the solitary confinement on death row would be enough to stop Gaskins from attempting to carry out another serious crime and possible murder they were dead wrong.

Weeks before Peewee was executed, a bizarre kidnapping plot was revealed that originated in prison with Gaskins once more being the mastermind.

In this plot Gaskins enlisted the help of some of his criminal colleagues to kidnap the daughter of prosecuting attorney Richard Harpootlian and hold her for ransom. Peewee's potential co-conspirators realized the gravity of the situation and quickly went to the authorities who then revoked most of the remaining privileges Peewee still had.

Peewee's last attempt at retribution and/or escape was thwarted. It was time for him to pay the piper.

A Familiar Companion

As Gaskins' execution date approached he was faced with the gravity of what he had done. Death was always something that followed Gaskins, it was a familiar friend; he was the grim reaper's right hand man for decades, but now the reaper was calling him.

Peewee's final words concerning death were somewhat defiant, but also megalomaniacal. "I am one of the few that truly understands what death and pain are all about," said Gaskins. "I have walked the same path as god. By taking lives and making others afraid of me, I become god's equal. Through killing others, I become my own master. Through my own power I come to my own redemption. Once I seen the miracle light, I didn't never again have to fear or obey the rule of no man or god."

For his execution, Gaskins was brought to the newly built Broad River Correctional Institute (BRCI), also known as the Capital Punishment Facility (CPF), outside Columbia, South Carolina.

Peewee's would be the second execution at BRCI and the only one in 1991.

On the day of his execution, September 6, 1991 Gaskins decided to take destiny into his own hands by cutting his wrists. The suicide attempt was unsuccessful as the prison authorities were able to quickly stitch him up and get him back to death row in time for his one a.m. execution.

The reason for Gaskins' suicide attempt remains unknown, but it probably had to do with one of the essential factors that drive most serial killers – control. By Gaskins own words he was not afraid of death as he stated: "I truly don't mind dying. I've lived a damned full and good life, and I don't believe there's much to death anyhow except peaceful darkness."

Gaskins did not fear death, he just wanted to have control over one more death!

After Gaskins was strapped into the electric chair he only said, "I'll let my lawyers talk for me, I'm ready to go."

And with that an electrical surge went through Gaskins body that ended the life of a monster.

South Carolina could breathe easier.

Chapter 8:

A Serial Killer Outlier

Earlier in this book, Professor David Wilson was quoted as saying that Donald Henry Gaskins would be a serial killer outlier if he killed as many people as he claimed. The reality is that the number of people Gaskins killed is not what made him an outlier, but it was the way he killed and the victims he chose – pathology and victimology – that made him a serial killer outlier.

A brief examination of Donald Gaskins' serial killer career compared to those of some other notable serial killers along with evidence compiled by experts in the field reveals that Peewee was a true outlier, which ultimately contributed to him possibly being the most dangerous and prolific serial killer in American history.

What is a Serial Killer?

The term *serial murderer* entered the mainstream lexicon in the late 1970s when FBI special agent Robert Ressler first used it to describe the perpetrator, David Berkowitz, in the "Son of Sam" killings. The FBI defines a serial killer as a person who, either alone or with an accomplice, kills at least three people over a period of time with a "cooling off" period between murders.

World history has been plagued with serial killers for centuries as accounts of their depraved deeds can be culled from ancient and medieval sources; but serial killers seem to have found their stride in modern times. Although serial killers have been found on every continent (aside from Antarctica) and nearly every country, they apparently feel particularly at home in the United States.

Beyond the basic definition, serial killers are actually quite diverse in terms of their pathologies and victimologies, although most tend not to deviate from a set pattern.

Numerous academic studies have been conducted over the last few decades in order to better understand the phenomenon of serial killers with one of the results being different systems of classification. Three of the most commonly used classification systems are the Deitz, Holmes, and Rappaport typologies, but several others also exist.

Peewee's Typology

Identifying Donald Henry Gaskins serial killer typology in order to determine if he was an outlier is not a simple task.

In order to do this Peewee's, murders should be divided into three categories: the coastal killings, the murder of friends and family, and the murders for hire and profit.

Gaskins' string of coastal killings, although disputed by many law enforcement officials, were clearly murders for pleasure and in Peewee's own words "weekend recreation." According to all of the major typologies Gaskins' coastal killings were indicative of a sexual sadist as he killed "for the sheer pleasure of torturing and murdering . . . in a sexual way," according to Laurence Miller.

By Gaskins' own words many of his coastal murders were spur of the moment events where he was taken over by the combination of his homicidal impulses and the convenience of a victim. These traits are more in line with a disorganized killer, although his often careful disposal of his victim's bodies indicates more forethought and organization.

The murders of Tyner, Bellamy, and others are defined by professionals as "utilitarian" killings and point towards, unlike the coastal killings, a fair amount of planning and organization. The Tyner murder especially was well organized and would have been difficult for someone with a low IQ to commit as Miller notes: "The best of them must possess keen intelligence and the ability to think quickly and flexibly and to restrain impulsive action." Despite being driven primarily by financial incentives, Miller points out that "some degree of narcissistic power thrill underlies these assassins' motivation for continuing in this line of work."

Finally, the "serious murders" that Gaskins committed on his friends and family falls into the sexual sadist typology. By all accounts Peewee raped and tortured his victims – such as Janice Kirby, Kim Ghelkins, and Doreen Dempsey – for sheer enjoyment and then disposed of their bodies in a partially organized manner.

Also, although Gaskins worked alone for the most part, he worked with others to carry out some of his profit killings, which in some ways sets him apart from other known serial killers.

A Comparative Study

Since Donald Henry Gaskins fits more than one type of serial killer typology it is difficult to compare him to other known serial killers. In terms of his coastal and "serious" killings he was clearly driven by an unnatural lust that culminated in necrophilia and cannibalism, which coincides with the pathology of Jeffery Dahmer, Ted Bundy and John Wayne Gacy.

Peewee differed from those three in his victimology. Although Peewee preferred women, he admitted that some of his coastal victims were boys and young men whom he sexually defiled in a manner similar to his female victims.

Gaskins' murders for profit also present an interesting case study when compared to other notable serial killers. Although most people usually do not think of contract killers as serial killers, they fit the FBI definition. One of the most prolific contract killers in American history was Richard Kuklinski, who may have killed over 200 men during his career.

Interviews with Kuklinski, nicknamed the "Iceman," revealed that he felt nothing – remorse or satisfaction – after his murders.

Kuklinski was driven purely by profit, while Gaskins had the twin urges of profit and sadism driving him.

Peewee also killed with partners from time to time, which is not unusual for serial killers. Perhaps one of the most famous serial killer tandems was the duo of Kenneth Bianchi and Angelo Buono, often known as the "Hillside Stranglers," who raped and murdered ten women in southern California during the late 1970s.

The difference between the Hillside Stranglers and Gaskins was that Gaskins never used partners for his sadistic killings, only for his profit murders.

Of all the best known serial killers, Gaskins' career most closely mirrored was that of Henry Lee Lucas. Lucas was convicted of murdering eleven people during the 1970s and '80s, but he confessed to hundreds more.

Lucas, like Gaskins, killed for both pleasure and profit and also used a partner for many of his murders. Also, Lucas killed men, women, and children like Gaskins.

A notable difference between the two serial killers though was that Gaskins kept most of his killings local, while Lucas travelled throughout the United States leaving a pile of bodies in his wake.

Ultimately it can be seen the Donald Henry Gaskins was a true serial killer outlier. His murders followed similar pathologies and victimologies to previous and later killers, but his killings spread throughout different categories and typologies, which would have made it difficult for law enforcement to capture him because they would not have known how many killers they were chasing.

That is what makes Donald Henry Gaskins one of the scariest serial killers in American history. In some ways he fit all of the stereotypes of what we think of as a serial killer, but in other ways he defied definition.

Experts believe that at any time there are approximately 200 to 500 serial killers operating at one time in the United States that account for 2000 to 3500 murders a year.

Those are scary numbers! Which one will be the next Donald Henry Gaskins?

Chapter 9:

The Legacy of Donald Henry "Peewee" Gaskins

Today, in the age of the internet it is interesting to put Donald Henry Gaskins' life into perspective. Gaskins hunted on the highways, backroads, and woods of South Carolina long before the internet existed and even before the FBI first coined the term "serial killer", but still his legacy persists.

Although Gaskins may not get top billing on most true crime television shows as one of America's top serial killers, the aura of his evil persists throughout South Carolina. Nearly every South Carolinian over the age of forty knows the name Donald Henry Gaskins and many have tales of how someone they know narrowly avoided the serial killer's murderous grip.

Peewee himself once said, "I think I been cheated because I'm not truly famous as I deserve to be."

In the highly connected internet age of today everyone has a chance to get their fifteen minutes of fame and for a lesser known serial killer like Donald Henry Gaskins it has been what he hoped for.

Gaskins now has a legion of fans and followers who can read about his deeds on his Facebook page or go to the conspiracy orientated website called "The Manifesto of Forbidden Truth" that touts him as a hero.

On the "Manifesto's" website Gaskins is described as one of many "underrated and unjustly obscure philosophers of truth" and "a tortured victim-creation of 20th century Amerikkkan society." The website displays many quotes by Gaskins and how they relate to some sort of esoteric knowledge.

The irony is obviously lost on the website's creator. Although Peewee would be delighted that his words and deeds live on through this website, he would be the last person to claim victimhood status.

Donald Henry Gaskins quit being a victim when he killed Hazel Brazell. After that he was a predator; possibly the worst predator in American history.

A Note From The Author

Hello, this is Jack Rosewood. Thank you reading Donald Gaskins: The Meanest Man In America. I hope you enjoyed the read of this chilling story. If you did, I'd appreciate if you would take a few moments to post a review on Amazon.

Best Regards

Jack Rosewood

Printed in Great Britain
by Amazon